Fear Not!
A DIVINE RESTRAINING ORDER *Against* the Spirit of Fear

ESTABLISHING A LEGAL FRAMEWORK IN
THE COURTS OF HEAVEN FOR LIVING A
FEARLESS LIFESTYLE IN TURBULENT TIMES!

Includes a Prayer of Activation

Against the Spirit of Fear

Dr. Francis Myles

© Copyright 2020 – Dr. Francis Myles

All rights reserved. This book is protected by the copyright laws of the United States of America. This book may not be copied or reprinted for commercial gain or profit. The use of short quotations or occasional page copying for personal or group study is permitted and encouraged. Permission will be granted upon request. Scripture quotations marked ESV are from The ESV® Bible (The Holy Bible, English Standard Version®). ESV® Text Edition: 2016. Copyright © 2001 by Crossway, a publishing ministry of Good News Publishers. The ESV® text has been reproduced in cooperation with and by permission of Good News Publishers. Unauthorized reproduction of this publication is prohibited. All rights reserved. Scripture quotations marked NKJV are from the New King James Version®. Copyright © 1982 by Thomas Nelson. Used by permission. All rights reserved. Scripture quotations marked TPT are from The Passion Translation®. Copyright © 2017 by Passion & Fire Ministries, Inc. Used by permission. All rights reserved. thePassionTranslation.com. Scripture quotations marked NLT are from the Holy Bible, New Living Translation, copyright © 1996, 2004, 2015 by Tyndale House Foundation. Used by permission of Tyndale House Publishers, Inc., Carol Stream, Illinois 60188. All rights reserved. Scripture quotations marked NIV are from THE HOLY BIBLE, NEW INTERNATIONAL VERSION®, NIV® Copyright © 1973, 1978, 1984, 2011 by Biblica, Inc.® Used by permission. All rights reserved worldwide.

All emphasis within Scripture quotations is the author's own.

DESTINY IMAGE® PUBLISHERS, INC.
PO Box 310, Shippensburg, PA 17257-0310
"Promoting Inspired Lives"

This book and all other Destiny Image and Destiny Image Fiction books are available at Christian bookstores and distributors worldwide.

For more information on foreign distributors, call 717-532-3040.

Or reach us on the Internet: www.destinyimage.com

ISBN 13 TP: 978-0-7684-5673-8

ISBN 13 eBook: 978-0-7684-5663-9

For Worldwide Distribution, Printed in the U.S.A.

1 2 3 4 5 6 / 23 22 21 20

Contents

Preface 7

Chapter 1 Fear Not! 11

Chapter 2 Leaning on Dead Branches 31

Chapter 3 How Satan Uses Your Fear in the Courts of Heaven 43

Chapter 4 Perfect Love Casts Out Fear! 61

Chapter 5 Prosecuting the Spirit of Fear in the Courts of Heaven 71

About the Author 81

Preface

Then He spoke a parable to them, that men always ought to pray and not lose heart.

— Luke 18:1

We are definitely living in the latter part of the period known as the End of Days! One of the signs of these end-of-days or the beginning of sorrows is the rising number of people who are paralyzed by fear and are on the verge of throwing in the towel! It is to this generation that Jesus says, "Men always ought to pray and not lose heart!"

Outbreaks such as the COVID-19 virus that has already killed thousands of people around the world and brought countries to the verge of total economic collapse has not helped calm people's minds—all this has done for many people is incite more of their fears.

Most importantly there are many members of the body of Messiah who are just as scared as the rest of the world. The only problem with the problem of fear is that it begets more fear, not less. In most cases there is nothing more dangerous than "fear itself." The day will come when we will look back at the outbreak of the coronavirus from the rearview mirror of history only to realize that our collective fear was a far more dangerous virus than the COVID-19 itself! This is so true.

Preface

This is why there are at least 366 recorded times in the Holy Bible where God says, "Fear not!" God does not want His people to live in fear. The writer of Proverbs tells us that the wicked run when there is nothing chasing them! What a picture of fear! On the other hand, the righteous are as bold as lion. Anyone who has seen a lion in its natural habitant knows it is afraid of nothing. It walks lazily by as though it owns the jungle and every animal in it! This is the picture that God wants painted in the canvas of our minds! When you are a child of God there is nothing to fear…more than the fear itself!

In this little booklet you will discover how satan uses "fear" to bind us in the Courts of Heaven. You will discover that in almost all cases of demonic bondage or entrapment, the driver the devil uses to open the doors of oppression is the spirit of fear! Fear has a paralyzing and chilling effect. This is why there have been cases when people died from a prank! Where comedy went horribly wrong, because the person on the receiving end of the prank convinced themselves of its veracity, even when in actuality everything was all make believe.

Needless to say, if fear is allowed to contaminate the mind, it is such a powerful and immobilizing force that some people never fully recover from it. This book contains a proven biblical model for living a fearless lifestyle. I encourage you to share this book with people or friends whom you know are struggling with fear.

Yours for His Kingdom,
Dr. Francis Myles
Author, *Issuing Divine Restraining Orders from the Courts of Heaven*
FrancisMyles.com

Chapter 1

Fear Not!

Fear not, for I am with you; be not dismayed, for I am your God. I will strengthen you, yes, I will help you, I will uphold you with My righteous right hand.

— *Isaiah 41:10*

Fear not! This expression appears in the canon of Scripture 366 times. Whichever way you slice this, God has a "Fear not" admonition for every person on earth for each day of the year! There is no other biblical admonition that comes close in its frequency to this admonition. What does God know about the destructive power of the "fear technology" that He wants to preserve us from? God certainly knows a whole lot about the destructive power of the spirit of fear.

In Hebraic tradition a truth is established at the testimony of two or three witness. What of something testified to 366 times in the Scriptures? The veracity of the expression "Fear not" is without question an established truth of Scripture. God does not want His people to live in "fear" regardless of the internal or external stimuli driving the fear. In God's economy, there is absolutely no reason to live in fear!

The Spirit of Fear

> *For God hath not given us the spirit of fear; but of power, and of love, and of a sound mind* (2 Timothy 1:7 KJV).

However, it behooves us to first understand "fear" itself, before we can master and conquer it. You have to admit that no one understands "fear" more than God. So His description of fear will be our underlying template for breaking the stronghold of fear over your life. Notice that God identifies fear as a spirit being, not just a mindset. If fear is a spirit being it means it can think, will, and act independently of its host. Notice that the Scripture says, *"For God hath not given us the spirit of fear."* This means that fear, like all other spirit beings, must be "received." Spirits cannot enter into a human being unless they have first been received. So if you are living in fear, it's because you already opened the door to the entrance of the spirit of fear. All spirits demand expression, including the Holy Spirit, so the spirit of fear will begin to project fearful thoughts in your mind in order to terrorize you further and find expression. With this understanding, it's impossible to be free from fear unless we are delivered from the spirit of fear. The last chapter of this book is designed to cast out the spirit of fear in your life.

Second Timothy 2:17 shows us what God has given us, namely—power, love, and a sound mind. This Scripture underpins why "fear" is so toxic spiritually and mentally. It takes three doses of the operation of God's

Spirit (power, love, and a sound mind) to overthrow the spirit of fear. So God has to infuse you and I with the spirit of power (*dunamis*), His unconditional love, and a sound mind in order to inoculate us from the fear. The good news is that because "fear" is an actual spirit being and not just a mindset, it can be prosecuted in the Courts of Heaven and cast out of your life in Jesus' name! In the last chapter of this book, I will show you how to prosecute the spirit of fear and issue a divine restraining order against it!

Twin Spirits: The Spirit of Fear and Death

> *Inasmuch then as the children have partaken of flesh and blood, He Himself likewise shared in the same, that through death He might destroy him who had*

the power of death, that is, the devil, and release those who through fear of death were all their lifetime subject to bondage (Hebrews 2:14-15).

Based upon the above Scripture, fear has a twin sister spirit called death. The Bible tells us that in dying Jesus destroyed the power of death, that is the devil. The resurrection of Jesus Christ is proof that there is a supernatural force more powerful than death. However, it is this second part of this verse that interests me the most. It shows a unique relationship between the spirit of fear and the spirit of death. The writer of Hebrews shows us that satan used the fear of death to force people on earth into a lifetime of bondage to the forces of darkness. In other words, it is fear that opens the door to every other spirit to invade your life. This passage of Scripture also shows us that being afraid of death does not stop it from coming; it increases the possibility that you're actually going to die. In other words, the fear of death opens the door to the spirit of death. You cannot have one without the other; they are twin spirits. It's no wonder the Bible tells us not to live in fear. When the coronavirus pandemic hit the globe, the fear of it killed more people than the virus itself. The global fear of the virus popularly known as COVID-19 caused billions of dollars in losses to the global economy. We will quickly examine the different types of fears that are mentioned in Scripture that God want us to be free from.

Types of Fear #1: The Fear of Death

And Abraham said, "Because I thought, surely the fear of God is not in this place;

and they will kill me on account of my wife" (Genesis 20:11).

One of the common fears mentioned in the Bible and that most people deal with on a daily basis is the fear of death. Everyone is afraid to die at some level. Death remains a mystery for the people on this planet, even though centuries of civilization have shown us that it is an inevitable occurrence. One way or the other, somebody is going to die, ever since Adam and Eve sinned against God in the garden of Eden and opened the door to the spirit of death. When Abraham arrived in Gerar, because he was afraid of being killed by the people of Gerar by reason of his wife's stunning beauty, he lied about the true nature of his relationship with his wife. He told them Sarah was his sister instead of his wife. So what was causing Abraham to place his wife in such a compromising situation? His fear of death. Even though he was a man of God, his fear of death had a tight grip on him. Sarah almost got sexually violated because of Abraham's fear. Thankfully, in the New Testament we don't have to be afraid of death because Jesus conquered death, hell, and the grave on the cross. Praise God!

Types of Fear #2: The Fear of Lack

> *And God heard the voice of the lad. Then the angel of God called to Hagar out of heaven, and said to her, "What ails you, Hagar? Fear not, for God has heard the voice of the lad where he is"* (Genesis 21:17).

Another equally universal fear of man is the fear of lack. This fear of lack has made thieves out of decent men and women. Correctional facilities all over the world are full of men and women who are in prison because satan deceived them to steal company or government funds, using their fear of lack. In the above passage of Scripture, Hagar was crying in a corner because she did not want to see the death of her child because of the lack of food or water. God chose this time to speak life into her spirit. According to Scripture, an angel of God called out to Hagar and said to her, *"Fear not, for God has heard the voice of the lad where he is."* It would seem to me that one of the many reasons most of us are afraid of lack is because we don't believe that God has heard our prayers for provision. Let me assure you! We don't serve a sleeping giant; we serve a mighty God who answers prayer at all times!

Types of Fear #3: The Fear of Failure

Only do not rebel against the Lord, nor fear the people of the land, for they are our bread; their protection has departed from them, and the Lord is with us. Do not fear them (Numbers 14:9).

The fear of failure is one of the most predominant fears that terrorizes the collective consciousness of the people of the planet. Who wants to fail, anyway? No one! This is because God designed us as winners! We were born to dominate this world and rule over every circumstance. However, life has taught us that sometimes even the most well-planned events or companies fail. This knowledge by itself has caused many people to live in the shadow of the fear of failure. In the above passage of Scripture, even though the twelve spies Moses sent to spy out the Promised Land discovered that the land was truly a land flowing with milk and honey, they were nevertheless afraid of losing a war to the giants they found in the land. Most people are so afraid of failure, they don't even try! If the last statement describes you, I say to you, in the name of Jesus Christ, fear not!

Types of Fear #4: The Fear of Ghosts or Demons

> *Now in the fourth watch of the night Jesus went to them, walking on the sea. And when the disciples saw Him walking on the sea, they were troubled, saying, "It is a ghost!" And they cried out for fear* (Matthew 14:25-26).

If most humans are like me, then they grew up with a background of folklore stories on ghosts and demons. Even though most humans are terrified of ghosts and demons, they are also intrigued by them. How else do we explain the horror movies that come out during Halloween or the costumes people wear during Halloween? The truth of the matter is that most often people are afraid of ghosts and demons. This explains the above passage of Scripture, where Jesus showed up walking on water toward His disciples and they went into panic mode. In their minds, no human being could walk on water. So what they were seeing had to be a ghost or a demon. With that kind of thinking controlling their minds, they were terrified. Jesus quickly identified Himself to them.

How many people have opened the door to a spirit of fear to control their life because of their fear of ghosts and demons? I believe it's countless thousands! To you I say, fear not!

Types of Fear #5: Imagined Fear

> *But immediately Jesus spoke to them, saying, "Be of good cheer! It is I; do not be afraid." And Peter answered Him and said, "Lord, if it is You, command me to come to You on the water." So He said, "Come." And when Peter had come down out of the boat, he walked on the water to go to Jesus. But when he saw that the wind was boisterous, he was afraid; and beginning to sink he cried out, saying, "Lord, save me!" And immediately Jesus stretched*

out His hand and caught him, and said to him, "O you of little faith, why did you doubt?" And when they got into the boat, the wind ceased (Matthew 14:27-32).

Of all the fears that man has to deal with, perhaps there is no fear more paralyzing and nonsensical than the fear of the unknown. I also call this kind of fear *imagined fear*. The psychologically disturbing effects of this type of fear know no bounds. This is because this fear is not based on logic, experience, or what's happening currently; it's purely speculative.

Peter saw Jesus walking on water. He clearly verified that it was Jesus. To further authenticate that the man walking on water was actually Jesus, Peter admonished the Lord to bid him to come and walk on water with Him. Jesus responded positively and said, "Come."

To his credit, Peter stepped out of the boat and began to walk on water. The first man in history other than Jesus to actually do so! Unfortunately, it did not last long. The reason was, Peter began to entertain imaginary fears about drowning in the water even though he was already walking on it. Once fear entered his heart, it ended his short-lived miracle. Jesus rebuked him for allowing his fears to get the best of him.

The Bible is full of the many different types of fears. What I have discussed in this book is not a comprehensive list of all the fears mentioned in the Bible. But it suffices to say that I can understand why God insists that His people restrain themselves from living in fear. God knows that fear is the number-one enemy to living in the Kingdom of God.

The Fear of the Lord

And He said, "Do not lay your hand on the lad, or do anything to him; for now I know that you fear God, since you have not withheld your son, your only son, from Me" (Genesis 22:12).

And Moses said to the people, "Do not fear; for God has come to test you, and that His fear may be before you, so that you may not sin" (Exodus 20:20).

Thankfully, the Bible also introduces us to the reverential fear of the Lord. This is the only fear encouraged in Scripture. I call the fear of the Lord the one fear that sets us free from all other fears! The fear of the Lord is the only fear that the Holy Spirit will ever introduce you to. This means that you must resist every other fear that is not the fear of the Lord. Every other fear will make you a subject or victim of bondage. Every other fear will terrorize your spirit and your mind, while the fear of the Lord will invigorate you.

Receive the Spirit of Life in Christ Jesus

> *There is therefore now no condemnation to those who are in Christ Jesus, who do not walk according to the flesh, but according to the Spirit. For the law of the Spirit of life in Christ Jesus has made me free from the law of sin and death* (Romans 8:1-2).

At the beginning of this chapter, we dissected 2 Timothy 1:7, which is says God has not given us a spirit of fear. I do not want you to forget the fact that all spirit-beings (divine or demonic) must be *received* before they can be *experienced*. Spirits don't just happen. They must first be received and then find expression in the life of the receiver. Just like operating in fear requires a person to receive the spirit of fear, there is also a spirit of life in Christ Jesus. The Spirit of life in Christ Jesus is far more powerful than the spirit of fear or the spirit of death! I want you to ask the Lord to fill you with the Spirit of life in Christ Jesus, which according to Scripture will make you free from the law of sin and death. Once you are free from the law of sin and death, fear will have no power over you!

Chapter 2

Leaning on Dead Branches

Thus says the Lord: "Cursed is the man who trusts in man and makes flesh his strength, whose heart departs from the Lord. For he shall be like a shrub in the desert, and shall not see when good comes, but shall inhabit the parched places in the wilderness, in a salt land which is not inhabited."

— Jeremiah 17:5-6

How many of us would be horrified if you saw a loved one holding on to a dead branch while standing at the edge of a cliff? In this chapter I will show you why I believe so many Christians or people of faith in general fail to live a fearless lifestyle. They are holding on to what legendary Christian writer E. Stanley Jones calls "leaning on dead branches." Dead branches represent anything that can be shaken that belongs to this world.

The prophet Jeremiah warns those of us holding on to dead branches. He declares in no uncertain terms: *"Cursed is the man who trusts in man and makes flesh his strength, whose heart departs from the Lord. For he shall be like a shrub in the desert, and shall not see when good comes, but shall inhabit the parched places in the wilderness, in a salt land which is not inhabited."* The prophet tells us that any human being who places his trust in the instruments of men or in his own genius is a man living under a curse. Such a person is easy pickings for the spirit of fear. All the devil has to do to frighten such a man or woman is to simply destroy the instruments of men that such a person idolizes.

They were several very influential and rich Americans who killed themselves when they realized that they had lost their financial fortunes to their trusted financial advisor by the name of Bernie Madoff. A chilling kind of fear crawled up their spine when they realized that the man they had trusted was actually running a Ponzi scheme. The spirit of fear entered their hearts and suffocated them to death! In the twinkling of an eye they realized that they had been leaning on "dead branches" and the branches had let them down!

Judas Hangs Himself

> *Then Judas, His betrayer, seeing that He had been condemned, was remorseful and brought back the thirty pieces of silver to the chief priests and elders, saying, "I have sinned by betraying innocent blood." And they said, "What is that to us? You see to it!" Then he threw down the pieces of silver in the temple and departed, and went and hanged himself* (Matthew 27:3-5).

We are living in a world where people have so many things they are hanging their hats on. Unfortunately, these things will let them down. Their trusted coat-hanger will fail them, and everything they hang on it will fall to the ground. When this happens, fear will envelope their soul, suffocating their hopes and dreams. In the above passage of Scripture, the Bible tells us about the story of Judas. It's a tragic tale indeed. He placed his faith in the almighty dollar instead of the living Lord. He made the mistake of trusting in what the Bible calls the deceitfulness of riches. He betrayed the Lord Jesus for 30 pieces of silver. However, when he received his reward it turned out to be stale bread! In his despondency he begged his fellow perpetrators to take back the 30 pieces of silver. If only the decision was that simple. When he realized, to his great dismay, that the consequences of his decision where irreversible, fear and a deep sense of helplessness engulfed his heart. He went and hanged himself. What a tragedy of biblical proportions!

The Connection Between Suicide and Fear

Then he threw down the pieces of silver in the temple and departed, and went and hanged himself (Matthew 27:5).

Based upon the above-mentioned Scripture, there is clearly a biblical connection as well as a psychological connection between the spirit of suicide and the spirit of fear. When Judas realized that the course of action his betrayal had unleashed was irreversible, both fear and helplessness got the best of him. Instead of running to Jesus to beg for forgiveness, the spirit of fear and hopelessness convinced him that there was no hope.

I've already shown you in the previous chapter that that the spirits of fear and death are twin sisters. You can't have one without the other. I asked the Lord, from His eternal perspective, what is the primary connection between suicide and fear? His response was refreshingly surprising. This is what He said: *"Francis, suicide is an intense fear to go on living. The person who commits suicide has been convinced by satan that the price of living far outweighs the price of dying."* I was stunned! The Lord was showing me that just like any other demonic spirit in the kingdom of darkness, the spirit of suicide waits for the spirit of fear to first do its job. As always, fear is the main driver and door opener. It's no wonder the Lord is screaming from the rooftops, "Fear not!"

I want to talk to anyone reading this book who is contemplating suicide. Like most suicides, thoughts to kill oneself come long before the suicide happens. Let me tell you unequivocally—the Lord wants you to live!

No matter what you have done, Jesus paid the price for your forgiveness. Don't let the devil convince you that the price of dying is a lesser price to pay than going on living. Even if you lost everything to the coronavirus or you've lost a loved one, Jesus wants you to know that there is more to your life than what you see currently. Don't kill yourself. God wants me to tell you that you shall live and not die and declare the glory of the Lord!

Everything Is Being Shaken!

Whose voice then shook the earth; but now He has promised, saying, "Yet once more I shake not only the earth, but also heaven." Now this, "Yet once more," indicates the removal of those things that are being shaken, as of things that are made, that the things which cannot be shaken may remain. Therefore, since we are receiving a kingdom which cannot be shaken, let us have grace, by which we may serve God acceptably with reverence and godly fear. For our God is a consuming fire (Hebrews 12:26-29).

Another main driver of fear in the last days is the fact that prophecies are being fulfilled. According to the writer of the book of Hebrews, in the above passage the Bible makes it clear that in the last days everything that can be shaken will be shaken. Everything that can be shaken in the heavens and on earth will be shaken before the second coming of Christ Jesus! Why? God does not want His people to be relying on anything that is man-made or demonically engineered. He wants all of His people and all of mankind to place their absolute faith in the finished work of Messiah-Jesus! Anything outside of the finished work of Christ is going to be shaken.

This includes positions of influence, jobs, businesses, careers, as well as relationships. God wants to remove every dead branch that has been giving us false hope. He will shake everything so that the dead branches can quickly disappoint us so that we may quickly lose our faith in every destructive, sinking sand that we had been holding on to. For the unprepared heart, this divine shaking is going to be a source of tremendous fear. Fear, because everything we held on to is being shaken. However, for those of us who choose to trust in Christ alone, we shall not be moved in the midst of the shaking. I hope and pray that this book can be used by the Lord to circumcise you from hanging your heart on dead branches.

Chapter 3

How Satan Uses Your Fear in the Courts of Heaven

*For the thing **I greatly feared** has come upon me, and what I dreaded has happened to me. I am not at ease, nor am I quiet; I have no rest, for trouble comes.*

— Job 3:25-26

Heaven has a very robust judicial system. Heaven houses many powerful courts of justice. Why? Because the Kingdom of Heaven is a sovereign government just like the United States or China. As a sovereign nation, the most powerful of them all, the Kingdom of Heaven has to have a Department of Justice. Moses tapped into this dimension of the Kingdom in order to bring the Ten Commandments as a system of law and jurisprudence into the earth realm. Have you noticed that all the law-abiding nations on earth have one version or another of the Ten Commandments? It is no wonder Moses is called the law-giver!

The Courts of Heaven

Before the Lord brought me into an understanding on the revelation of operating in the Courts of Heaven, the following passage from the book of Job was a very difficult passage of Scripture for me to handle. The Bible is very clear that lucifer (satan) and the angels that fell with him were cast out of Heaven. They fell into the earth realm like lightening! This is what Jesus said in the New Testament. So what in God's name was satan doing in Heaven? Why is he standing before the Lord? For the most part, I ignored the obvious theological quagmire hidden in the passage. I just believed it by faith, even though the theologian in me remained unsettled.

> *Now there was a day when the sons of God came to present themselves before the Lord, and Satan also came among them. And the Lord said to Satan, "From where do you come?" So Satan answered the Lord and said, "From going to and fro on the earth, and from*

walking back and forth on it." Then the Lord said to Satan, "Have you considered My servant Job, that there is none like him on the earth, a blameless and upright man, one who fears God and shuns evil?" So Satan answered the Lord and said, "Does Job fear God for nothing? Have You not made a hedge around him, around his household, and around all that he has on every side? You have blessed the work of his hands, and his possessions have increased in the land. But now, stretch out Your hand and touch all that he has, and he will surely curse You to Your face!" And the Lord said to Satan, "Behold, all that he has is in your power; only do not lay a hand on his person." So Satan went out from the presence of the Lord (Job 1:6-12).

After years of intensive study of the Bible and after meeting my dear friend Robert Henderson, the light bulb of revelation suddenly flooded my soul! This passage of Scripture from the book of Job no longer posed a theological dilemma. It made perfect sense! Satan has been cast out of Heaven just like the Bible says. However, the Lord himself is a pragmatist. He knows that until this dispensation of sin has been concluded, mankind is responsible for the actions they take for or against the Word of God. In the event that the Word of God has been broken or violated and a spiritual crime committed, so to speak, there would be a need for a heavenly judicial system to handle these matters of law. That being the case, no self-respecting judge can allow a trial to proceed without first making sure that the defense and prosecutorial tables are seated. So in the courts of Heaven, satan plays the role of the prosecutor or accuser of the brethren. The Greek word for "accuser" literally means "one who brings a lawsuit." You and I know that the only place to effectively adjudicate a lawsuit is inside a courtroom. You cannot adjudicate a lawsuit inside a church; you need a courtroom.

I suddenly noticed that in this passage from the book of Job, God never asked satan to explain why he was in Heaven. This would have been the most obvious question, if satan has no legal rights of any kind to visit the heavenly kingdom after his expulsion. However, that is not the question that the Lord asked. Instead, He asked satan to explain where on earth he was coming from. The passage also shows that satan was in Heaven to present cases (containing spiritual crimes committed by the children of men). Satan was in heaven to "accuse" or bring lawsuits against the children of men from evidence collected by traveling back and forth on earth.

The Divine Restraining Order

It is within this judicial context that the story of Job takes a turn. Before hearing the cases satan had brought to court, the Lord proceeded to talk about His servant Job. God said to satan:

> *"Have you considered My servant Job, that there is none like him on the earth, a blameless and upright man, one who fears God and shuns evil?" So Satan answered the Lord and said, "Does Job fear God for nothing? Have You not made a hedge around him, around his household, and around all that he has on every side? You have blessed*

the work of his hands, and his possessions have increased in the land. But now, stretch out Your hand and touch all that he has, and he will surely curse You to Your face!" And the Lord said to Satan, "Behold, all that he has is in your power; only do not lay a hand on his person." So Satan went out from the presence of the Lord (Job 1:8-12).

In judicial terms, the Lord asked satan this question. "Have you investigated Job? That there is no one like him on the earth." To which satan replied, "Does Job fear God for nothing? Have You not made a hedge around him, around his household, and around all that he has on every side?" Interestingly enough, the word *hedge* actually comes from the Hebrew word *skuwk*, meaning a "restraint." Placing satan's complaint in judicial terms, this is what satan was saying: "Have You not placed a divine restraining order around him, around his household, and around all that he has on every side?" Thus, the divine protection around Job was legal in nature. Anyone familiar with the legal profession knows that restraining orders are "protective orders" of the court.

Finding Satan's Legal Entry

There was a man in the land of Uz, whose name was Job; and that man was blameless and upright, and one who feared God and shunned evil. And seven sons and three daughters were born to him. Also, his possessions were seven thousand sheep, three thousand camels, five hundred yoke of oxen, five hundred female donkeys, and a very large household, so that this man was the greatest of all the people of the East. And his sons would go and feast in their houses, each on his appointed day, and would send and invite their three sisters to eat and drink with them. So it was, when the days of feasting had run their course, that Job would send and sanctify them, and he would rise early in the morning and offer burnt offerings according to the number of them all. For Job said, "It may be that my sons have sinned and cursed God in their hearts." Thus Job did regularly (Job 1:1-5).

For the longest time, I was also troubled by why God even brought up Job's name in the first place. It's clear from the text that satan had not come into the Court of Heaven to place Job on trial. So why would God bring up Job when satan was clearly not after him? This bothered me for quite a while until I discovered God's redemptive purpose. When examining the first verses in the book of Job, the Bible is clear that God had blessed Job tremendously. Job was a righteous man who feared God and shunned any kind of evil. The Lord was very pleased with him. However, it was clear as well from the text that Job was also living in fear. I believe the Lord was using the story of Job to illustrate how even people who love God, fear Him, and shun evil can still open a door that gives the devil legal entry into their life. This seems to be the case with Job. Let us examine the following Scripture.

> *For the thing **I greatly feared** has come upon me, and what I dreaded has happened to me. I am not at ease, nor*

am I quiet; I have no rest, for trouble comes (Job 3:25-26).

According to this passage of Scripture, even though Job loved and feared the Lord, Job had another kind of fear that was competing with the fear of the Lord. Using Job's own words, he describes this "fear" as "the thing I greatly feared." It would seem that whatever this fear was, it was in some respects equal or greater to the fear of the Lord. By definition, anything that competes with the Lord is an idol. And idols give satan legal entry into our life and room to bring legal accusations against us in the Courts of Heaven. Apparently, this thing Job greatly feared had become an idol and the Lord wanted it destroyed.

Apparently, satan knew that this fear was there too, but the only thing that was keeping satan from attacking Job's life due to this open door was the "hedge" or divine restraining order that God had placed on Job's life, his family, and everything he owned. This is why satan argued for its immediate removal. As soon as God removed the divine restraining order that was keeping satan from attacking Job because of his living in fear, satan wasted no time in exploiting the legal entry. He moved in for the kill!

The Thing I Greatly Feared!

> *So it was, when the days of feasting had run their course, that Job would send and sanctify them, and he would rise early in the morning and offer burnt offerings according to the number of them all. For Job said, "It may be that*

my sons have sinned and cursed God in their hearts." Thus Job did regularly (Job 1:5).

So, what is the thing that Job greatly feared? The above passage of Scripture shows us that the thing Job greatly feared was that his children would sin against God and die. Job was living in dreadful anticipation that one fateful day his beloved children would curse God in their hearts and then die. For the wages of sin is death (see Rom. 6:23). Consequently, the possible death of his children due to them sinning against God kept him up at night. In his own words, Job says he could not rest over this issue. In other words, no amount of time spent in God's presence could release him from this fear! He felt like it was up to him to keep his children from falling from grace. *Never mind that the Lord is the only One who can keep us from falling.* To that extent Job's fear caused him to do the Lord's work. In a sense, Job was acting as though he was the blessed Holy Spirit, charged with the sacred work of convicting the world of sin, righteousness, and judgment. Instead of rescuing his children, what did Job get? He got the very thing he feared the most—*the sudden death of his children!* So even in Job's life, fear did not bring life but certain death. *Most importantly, the hidden lesson here is that idolizing your children never brings you peace, just fear and a restless spirit.*

> *While he was still speaking, another also came and said, "Your sons and daughters were eating and drinking wine in their oldest brother's house, and suddenly a great wind came from across the wilderness and struck the four corners of the house, and it fell on*

the young people, and they are dead; and I alone have escaped to tell you! (Job 1:18-19)

Please remember the fear of death comes before the spirit of death. It's exactly what happened to Job. If you're afraid of losing your job, more often than not you're going to lose your job. If you're afraid of dying, more often than not dying is what you're going to get. If you're afraid of financial bankruptcy, the chances are it's what you're going to get. If you're afraid of catching a virus or a certain disease, more often than not you will get what you fear the most! *The moral of the story of Job is that we tend to get the thing we fear the most.* Satan used Job's fear against him in the courts of Heaven. It's no wonder the Lord does not want His people to live in fear. Even though Job loved the Lord, it is clear the thing he feared the most made it difficult for him to rest in the Lord his God. Maybe this last statement describes you. What are you going to do about it? It's time to take all your fears into the Court of Heaven and prosecute them before they destroy your life. *So fear not!*

Chapter 4

Perfect Love Casts Out Fear!

He who does not love does not know God, for God is love.

— 1 John 4:8

To me the whole Bible is one gigantic, unending saga of divine romance! Even the moments of divine judgement, such as the destruction of Sodom and Gomorrah, when you actually peel the onion you quickly discover that everything the Lord did was for our ultimate good. Hatred as a principle lives not in the heart of the God who is Love itself. All you need to do is read the Song of Solomon or look at the face and battered body of Jesus on the Cross to realize that whoever God is, love and not hate is what motivates Him!

It's no wonder the writer of the book of John declares beautifully, *"He who does not love does not know God, for God is love."* If anyone is not motivated by love in his or her ministry or service, they do not know God, for God is love. *Pure, unadulterated Love, without spot or wrinkle.* This is the love of the God who sent His only begotten Son, Messiah-Jesus, to die for us on the Cross. So how can we live in fear in a world created and controlled by such a benevolent and loving Creator? This leads me to the following passage—my absolute favorite passage of Scripture. The whole philosophy of living a fearless lifestyle hangs on the following passage of Scripture. Without it we would have no reason to hope.

Casting Out Fear!

> *Love has been perfected among us in this: that we may have boldness in the day of judgment; because as He is, so are we in this world. There is no fear in love; but perfect love casts out fear, because fear involves torment. But he who fears has not been made perfect in love. We love Him because He first loved us* (1 John 4:17-19).

The apostle John gives us a litmus test to authenticate the fact that we have become perfected or matured in the love of God. He says when our understanding of the love of God is perfected, we will lose all fear of the day of judgment. Why is this such a beautiful expression of maturing in the love of God? I believe it's because the reason most humans live in fear is because they don't know what awaits them on the other side of the grave. Perhaps there is no fear more terrifying than the possibility of spending eternity in hell, eternally lost and separated from God. This fact alone terrifies most humans. *However, Jesus died and paid a heavy price to rescue us from spending eternity separated from the presence and love of God.*

If you have received the Lord Jesus as your personal Lord and Savior, you have no reason to live in fear! *Fear of the afterlife is no longer your portion.* Messiah-Jesus defeated sin, the grave, hell, and the devil so you and I can have eternal life! Eternal life begins on earth the moment you receive Messiah-Jesus as your personal Lord and Savior. *"These things I have written to you who believe in the name of the Son of God, that you may know that you have eternal life, and that you may continue to believe in the name of the Son of God"* (1 John 5:13). In other words, eternal life breaks the power the devil had over us through the fear of death.

However, it is the following verse that places a death nail in the coffin of living in fear. The apostle John declares, *"There is no fear in love; but perfect love casts out fear, because fear involves torment. But he who fears has not been made perfect in love"* (1 John 4:18). He makes a beautiful statement that there is absolutely no fear in the love of God. When you and I encounter the true love of God, it will destroy every trace of fear in our heart. Most importantly, the apostle John declares the perfect love of God casts out all fear. What is interesting is the apostle John's usage of the words cast out. These are words the Bible uses to describe an exorcism. The casting out of an actual demonic entity with both feelings and personality. This expression cast out is used a lot in the ministry of the Lord Jesus to describe the actual exorcism of a spirit being out of a person who was oppressed by it: *"And these signs will follow those who believe: In My name they will **cast out** demons; they will speak with new tongues"* (Mark 16:17).

With this understanding, let us once again examine what the apostle John is saying: *"Perfect love casts out fear."* He is deliberately using this expression to make abundantly clear that what the perfect love of God wants to cast out of all of His children is the spirit of fear itself! The spirit entity that is responsible for driving the machinery of fear in the kingdom of darkness is what the love of God wants to expel. *The perfect love of God is so strong, so overpowering that the principality of fear itself is no match for the perfect love of God!* Hallelujah!

Fear Has Torment

> *There is no fear in love; but perfect love casts out fear, because fear involves torment. But he who fears has not been made perfect in love* (1 John 4:18).

The apostle John goes even further to explain why God does not want His children to live in fear. He says, *"because fear involves torment. But he who fears has not been made perfect in love."* There it is! Fear that is demonically engineered always involves the desire to torment the person held in captivity by the thing they fear. God is not a tormentor! God is a lover! On the other hand, satan is a tormentor. He loves to torment people. He loves to see people suffer. None of these things excite the Lord, because He is the one who created you. He created you and I to be loved and to live in peace and harmony with Him. He created us to glory in His glorious presence. Thankfully, Jesus died to make all of this possible again. So I say to you, "Fear not!"

Discerning of Spirits

Beloved, do not believe every spirit, but test the spirits, whether they are of God; because many false prophets have gone out into the world. By this you know the Spirit of God: Every spirit that confesses that Jesus Christ has come in the flesh is of God, and every spirit that does not confess that Jesus Christ has come in the flesh is not of God. And this is the spirit of the Antichrist, which you have heard was coming, and is now already in the world (1 John 4:1-3).

Based upon what the apostle John just told us in 1 John 4:18, it's no wonder he warns us not to believe every spirit but to test every spirit to determine whether they are from God or from the very pit of hell. He wants us to discern the spirits that are coming into our environment or touching our spirit and mind. Why does he give us this warning? Because he knows that the spirit of the antichrist has already gone out into the world. These antichrist spirits do not want you and I to experience the glories of Heaven that the Lord Jesus Christ purchased on the Cross. Instead, these malicious spirits want to stop us from experiencing the agape love of God and the life of the Lord Jesus Christ. I believe one of the main reasons some Christians live in perpetual fear is because they don't take the time to test the spirits that are touching their minds. It's time to discern these spirits and say "No" to living in fear, in Jesus' mighty name! Hallelujah!

Chapter 5

Prosecuting the Spirit of Fear in the Courts of Heaven

Prayer of Activation

For God hath not given us the spirit of fear; but of power, and of love, and of a sound mind.
— *2 Timothy 1:7 KJV*

Heavenly Father and righteous Judge, thank You for allowing me to address the Courts of Heaven. I have come to receive Your righteous judgment over my life concerning matters of destiny that directly affect me and the Kingdom of God. Heavenly Father, I am standing before Your royal and supreme court because of the shed blood and finished work of Yeshua (Jesus) on the cross. Heavenly Father, in all humility, I ask that the Courts of Heaven be seated according to Daniel 7:10. I ask this in Jesus' mighty name. Heavenly Father, I call upon Your holy angels to be witnesses to this legal and righteous transaction. I also decree and declare that the spirit of fear that will be impacted directly by the divine restraining order that I am requesting will be duly notified by Your holy angels who service the Courts of Heaven, in Jesus' name I pray. Heavenly Father, I decree and declare that spirit of fear, which has been tormenting me, will be cast out and abide by Your righteous judgment, in Yeshua's mighty name.

Heavenly Father, it is written, *"For God hath not given us the spirit of fear; but of power, and of love, and of a sound mind."* Heavenly Father, I repent for bowing my knees to the spirit of fear and allowing it to control my life. Like Job, I repent, Lord, for allowing the things that I fear the most to compete with the fear of the Lord in my life. Heavenly Father, forgive me for idolizing my fears! Heavenly Father, it is written in 1 John 1:9, *"If we confess our sins, He is faithful and just to forgive us our sins and to cleanse us from all unrighteousness."* Heavenly Father, I ask that You wash away all my sins and my fears in Jesus' mighty name. Thank You for cleansing me from all unrighteousness!

Heavenly Father, even as I stand in Your royal courtroom I present myself as a living sacrifice, holy and acceptable before You according to Romans 12:1. Lord, I ask that any place in me that is displeasing to You, that is unrighteous before You, would be unveiled so I can repent of it. Holy Spirit, let the blood of Yeshua/Jesus speak on my behalf in Heaven, on earth, and in the underworld. Lord Jesus, I am sorry for all my sins and transgressions; cleanse me by Your precious blood so satan has no legal footing to resist the divine restraining order against the spirit of fear that I need from Your heavenly Courtroom.

Heavenly Father, I repent for personal transgressions as well as for the iniquities of my ancestral bloodline that may have opened a door for the spirit of fear to come after my life. Righteous Judge, may every sin and iniquity of my forefathers that satan has been using as a legal foothold to bring accusations against me in the court of Heaven be revoked by the blood of Jesus. It is written that a "curse causeless will never arise." I ask that that any other legal right the spirit of fear is holding on to be revoked in Yeshua's glorious name. Let the all the chains of fear be removed from my life.

Heavenly Father, I present before Your Supreme Court the following Scriptures as irrefutable evidence against the operation of the spirit of fear and death in my life.

It is written:

For God has not given us a spirit of fear, but of power and of love and of a sound mind (2 Timothy 1:7)

You shall not be afraid of the terror by night, nor of the arrow that flies by day, Nor of the pestilence that walks in darkness, nor of the destruction that lays waste at noonday.

A thousand may fall at your side, and ten thousand at your right hand; but it shall not come near you. Only with your eyes shall you look, and see the reward of the wicked.

Because you have made the Lord, who is my refuge, even the Most High, your dwelling place, no evil shall befall you, nor shall any plague come near your dwelling (Psalm 91:5-10).

The wicked flee when no one pursues, But the righteous are bold as a lion (Proverbs 28:1).

Heavenly Father, based upon the aforementioned Scriptures, it is clear that if your Supreme Court does not grant me a *divine restraining order* against the spirit of fear, the kingdom of darkness will cause great injury to my life, destiny, as well as inflict irreparable damage to the purposes of God. Righteous Judge, far it be from You not to do what is right, and what is right and just is for You to deliver me from the clutches of the spirit of fear for the sake of Your only begotten Son, the Lord Jesus Christ.

Heavenly Father, I now ask that *a divine restraining order against the spirit of fear and all its sister spirits would **now** be issued on my behalf from Your Supreme Court, in Yeshua's glorious name. Heavenly Father, I receive this divine restraining order by faith, in Jesus' name, for without faith it is impossible to please God. Righteous Judge, it is written in the book of Psalms, "Bless the Lord, you His angels, who excel in strength, who do His word, heeding the voice of His word"* (Ps. 103:20). I therefore make a motion that You assign high-ranking angelic officers of the Courts of Heaven to officiate the enforcement of this divine restraining order against the spirit of fear. I also decree that these high-ranking angelic officers of the Courts of Heaven will hold the spirit of fear in contempt of court should this spirit make any attempt to violate this divine restraining order. In Yeshua's name I pray. Amen!

Prayer Adapted from *Issuing Divine Restraining Orders from the Courts of Heaven* by Dr. Francis Myles, published by Destiny Image. Used with permission, francismyles.com.

About the Author

DR. FRANCIS MYLES is a multi-gifted international motivational speaker, business consultant, and apostle to the nations. He is the senior pastor of Lovefest Church International in Tempe, Arizona. He is also the creator and founder of the world's first Marketplace BibleTM. He is a sought after conference speaker in both ministerial and marketplace seminars. Dr. Myles is also a spiritual life coach to movers and shakers in the marketplace and political arena. He has appeared on TBN, God-TV, and Daystar. He has been a featured guest on Sid Roth's *It's Supernatural!* TV show.

Dr. Myles is happily married to the love of his life, Carmela Real Myles, and they reside in the Phoenix Metroplex, in the state of Arizona.

Experience a personal revival!

Spirit-empowered content from today's top Christian authors delivered directly to your inbox.

Join today!
lovetoreadclub.com

Inspiring Articles
Powerful Video Teaching
Resources for Revival

Get all of this and so much more, e-mailed to you twice weekly!

LOVE TO READ CLUB
by **DESTINY IMAGE**

Printed in Great Britain
by Amazon